MW00724073

A Special Gift

presented to:

_____

from:

_____

date:

_____

a little book of

hugs™

to
encourage
and inspire

Inspiration for the Heart

HOWARD
PUBLISHING CO.

A Little Book of Hugs to Encourage and Inspire
© 2000 by Howard Publishing Co., Inc.
All rights reserved. Printed in China

Published by Howard Publishing Co., Inc.,
3117 North 7th Street, West Monroe, LA 71291-2227

00 01 02 03 04   5 4 3 2 1

ISBN: 1-58229-120-9

Messages by G. A. Myers
Paraphrased Scriptures by LeAnn Weiss
Interior design by Vanessa Bearden
Project Editor: Philis Boultinghouse

Contents

The spirit, the will to win, and the will to excel are the things that endure. These qualities are so much more important than the events that occur.

—*Vince Lombardi*

the
POWER
of
Giving

Don't be selfish
or self-seeking in
anything that you do.

Instead of being self-promoting,
be *humble*
and *consider others*
MORE *important*
than yourself in
all you do and *say*.

Encourage
one another,
and *build*
each other UP.

Love,
Jesus

Philippians 2:3; 1 Thessalonians 5:11

When was the last time you felt really warm and loved?
Think about it.

It was probably the last
time someone went out of
his or her way to do or say
something nice to you—
something unrequested,
out of the blue, just
because—something that
made you feel valued and
appreciated.

5

And that's how you can make others feel loved—by doing or saying something nice...just because.

So give of yourself
and of your time; give
surprise gifts and
encouraging words.

Take your spouse on a date and focus all your attention on your chosen one. Gather your family around the kitchen table and initiate an appreciation session. Take a friend to lunch just to remind him or her that you cherish that relationship.

Giving is the spark that
ignites the fires of love.
You have the power to
start a blazing fury of
selfless love.

Maturity begins to grow when you can sense your concern for others outweighing your concern for yourself.

—*John McNaughton*

c h a p t e r   t w o

the
FREEDOM
of *Forgiveness*

13

Good News! Everyone who *believes* in **Me** receives TOTAL *forgiveness* of *sin* through My name.

There isn't *any* CONDEMNATION. Because of what I did at **Calvary**, you've been set *free* from the law of **SIN** *and* **DEATH**.

Your record
has been *wiped* CLEAN.
I *forgive*
and *forget!*

Love,

*Your Forgiving
and Forgetting Savior*

Acts 10:43;
Romans 8:1–2; Hebrews 10:17

"*You* are forgiven."
Just words? No—much more. The mere utterance of these three little words can free prisoners from guilt in an instant.

*S*ay the words quietly
to yourself, then speak
them boldly to needy
souls around you.

*G*raciously accepting
the forgiveness freely
given to us by God, we
are compelled to become
conduits of forgiveness
for others.

*S*omeone near you
needs forgiveness today.
You hold the power to
free that person.

If the offense was committed against you, remember your own undeserved forgiveness; draw from that abundant supply and share what has been given to you— it is not yours to hoard.

If the offense is against someone else, speak a word of testimony about God's loving forgiveness and encourage actions that lead to healing.

Forgiveness releases others from their indebtedness to us and releases us from our indebtedness to them— both freed to love.

You have been given a precious power. Receive and give it generously and often.

Our God has
a big eraser.

—*Billy Zeoli*

How magnificent is grace! How sweet are the promises! How sour is the past! How precious and broad is God's love! How petty and narrow are man's limitations! How refreshing is the Lord!

—*Charles Swindoll*

chapter three

3

the
SECRET
of
Acceptance

Practice **humility**
toward one another.

I *oppose* the **PROUD**.

But I give My
A M A Z I N G
grace
to those
who are HUMBLE.

Love,
Your God Who Is Gentle
and Humble in Heart

I'm going to tell you
a secret that will make
you feel a whole lot
better about yourself.

It's something you've allowed yourself to consider before...but not for very long.

The very essence of this secret will make you bristle, even though you know that accepting it will ease your mind, calm your spirit, and even whet your appetite for growth.

Are you ready? I know you can handle it, though not everyone can. Here goes:

You are not always right.

$\mathcal{I}$ saw you smile,
because you know I'm
right—well, about this,
anyway.

Trying to be right about
everything is a load you
cannot carry, and the cost
is far more than you can
afford.

The next time you look in the mirror, you may want to remind yourself of this secret.

And I'll tell you
another secret: Admitting
that you're not always
right makes you even more
lovable than you already
are—if that's possible.

God created the
world out of nothing,
and so long as we are
nothing, he can make
something out of us.

—Martin Luther

chapter four

the
ESSENCE
of *Courage*

Be full of STRENGTH
and *courage*.

Do not be *terrified*;

do not be discouraged.
I will be *with you*
wherever
you go.

Love,
  Your God of
Strength and Courage

Joshua 1:9

Would you
describe yourself as a
person of courage?
Probably not.

*Y*our image of courage
may have been shaped by
television and movies:
Courage is Superwoman
flying to rescue a helpless
child from a burning
building.

Or perhaps it's Will Smith saving the world from aliens who plan to destroy us and confiscate our natural resources.

*M*ake-believe courage
is hard to live up to. But
real courage, in real life,
may describe you to a tee.

It takes courage to care about family and friends enough to get involved with their struggles. It takes courage to complete what you start. It takes courage to confront weakness in your own life and in the lives of those you love.

It takes courage to confess that your thoughtless words or negligent actions have hurt someone you love. Quite simply, it takes courage to live each day with integrity.

*Y*ou may not describe
yourself as a person of
courage, but look again—
you may discover
courageous feats of
kindness or heroic
manifestations of
unconditional love.

*S*ay, would you like
to be in a movie?

Courage is
fear that has said
its prayers.

—from
One Day at a Time,
Al-Anon

chapter five

the RICHES
of *Memories*

I want you to think about
whatever is **true**.

Think about things that are
NOBLE or *RIGHT*…
things that are
pure *and lovely*.

Reflect upon
ADMIRABLE qualities and
memories.

Remember
whatever is
EXCELLENT or
praiseworthy.

Love,
  Your God of Every
Good and Perfect Gift

Philippians 4:8

You may not
realize it, but you are
a rich person. Yes, you!
You possess a huge vault
brimming with treasure,
and you can withdraw
assets from this vault
whenever you want—at
absolutely no cost.

Where is this vault?
It is inside the caverns
of your heart and mind.
And what treasure
resides there?
　Memories.

$\mathcal{M}$emories are pictures of past events and people that powerfully affect your present and future. There are those funny memories from long ago that make you laugh, even now.

Then there are those
embarrassing memories
that flash through your
mind at the oddest times,
even causing you to blush.

But there are certain kinds of memories that glisten like diamonds. They remind you that your life is rich with meaning and purpose—that you matter to other people and that other people matter to you.

$\mathcal{M}$emories of special moments when love was exchanged and cherished, when a significant relationship took a big step forward, when delicious laughter cheered your soul—these precious memories are all waiting for you to pick them up, dust them off, and bring them to life once again.

So when your heart is heavy or you're feeling all alone, open the door…go ahead. Dig in. Make all the withdrawals you want.

You can't deplete the supply. In fact, you may find that you are so rich you can loan some of your wealth to others.

Enjoy yourself.
These are the good
old days you are going
to miss in ten years.

—*Unknown*

Trust the past to God's mercy, the present to his love, and the future to his providence.

—*St. Augustine*

Look for these other little *Hugs* books:

A Little Book of Hugs for Friends
A Little Book of Hugs for Sisters
A Little Book of Hugs for Women
A Little Book of Hugs for Teachers
A Little Book of Hugs for Mom

Also look for these full-size *Hugs* books:

Hugs for Women
Hugs for Friends
Hugs for Mom
Hugs for Kids
Hugs for Teachers
Hugs for Sisters
Hugs for Those in Love
Hugs for the Hurting
Hugs for Grandparents
Hugs for Dad
Hugs for the Holidays
Hugs to Encourage and Inspire